Clownfish and sea anemones
JNF Animals Behavior

Medi.

AR: 3.0
Pts: 0.5

DISCARDED

DATE DUE

2/20

FEB 1 9 2020			
			PRINTED IN U.S.A.

DISCARDED

Clownfish
and
Sea Anemones

by Kari Schuetz

BELLWETHER MEDIA • MINNEAPOLIS, MN

Note to Librarians, Teachers, and Parents:

Blastoff! Readers are carefully developed by literacy experts and combine standards-based content with developmentally appropriate text.

Level 1 provides the most support through repetition of high-frequency words, light text, predictable sentence patterns, and strong visual support.

Level 2 offers early readers a bit more challenge through varied simple sentences, increased text load, and less repetition of high-frequency words.

Level 3 advances early-fluent readers toward fluency through increased text and concept load, less reliance on visuals, longer sentences, and more literary language.

Level 4 builds reading stamina by providing more text per page, increased use of punctuation, greater variation in sentence patterns, and increasingly challenging vocabulary.

Level 5 encourages children to move from "learning to read" to "reading to learn" by providing even more text, varied writing styles, and less familiar topics.

Whichever book is right for your reader, Blastoff! Readers are the perfect books to build confidence and encourage a love of reading that will last a lifetime!

This edition first published in 2019 by Bellwether Media, Inc.

No part of this publication may be reproduced in whole or in part without written permission of the publisher. For information regarding permission, write to Bellwether Media, Inc., Attention: Permissions Department, 6012 Blue Circle Drive, Minnetonka, MN 55343.

Library of Congress Cataloging-in-Publication Data

Names: Schuetz, Kari, author.
Title: Clownfish and Sea Anemones / by Kari Schuetz.
Description: Minneapolis, MN : Bellwether Media, Inc., [2019] | Series:
   Blastoff! Readers. Animal Tag Teams | Audience: Ages 5-8. | Audience: K to
   grade 3. | Includes bibliographical references and index.
Identifiers: LCCN 2018033933 (print) | LCCN 2018034867 (ebook) | ISBN
   9781681036847 (ebook) | ISBN 9781626179547 (hardcover : alk. paper)
Subjects: LCSH: Mutualism (Biology)–Juvenile literature. |
   Anemonefishes–Behavior–Juvenile literature. | Sea
   anemones–Behavior–Juvenile literature. | Reef ecology–Juvenile
   literature.
Classification: LCC QL638.G7 (ebook) | LCC QL638.G7 S37 2019 (print) | DDC
   577.8/52–dc23
LC record available at https://lccn.loc.gov/2018033933

Editor: Betsy Rathburn   Designer: Brittany McIntosh

Printed in the United States of America, North Mankato, MN

Table of Contents

Becoming Friends

A clownfish swims up to a sea anemone. This fish is looking for a friend.

To say hello, it dances
around the anemone.
It uses touch to create
a lasting connection!

Clownfish and sea anemones live together in crowded **coral reefs**. Those in the Pacific and Indian Oceans become friends to survive.

Tag Team Range

= clownfish and sea anemone range

The **symbiosis** between these animals brings many benefits.

Clownfish are small fish with a bold look. Many have bright orange bodies with white bands.

Black coloring borders the bands. A coat of **mucus** protects the fish's scales.

Common Clownfish Profile

type: **fish**

size: **4.3 inches (11 centimeters) long**

life span: **6 to 10 years**

The fish catch mini meals
with their little mouths.
As **omnivores**, they eat
tiny plants and animals.

Predators such as sharks see the fish as easy **prey**. They hunt the slow-swimming clownfish.

Flowers of the Sea

tentacles

Sea anemones are **invertebrates** with a flowery appearance.

Tentacles reach out from their soft bodies like petals from a flower. These body parts are full of **venom**!

Bubble Tip Sea Anemone Profile

type: **invertebrate**

size: **12 inches (30 centimeters) wide**

life span: **more than 50 years**

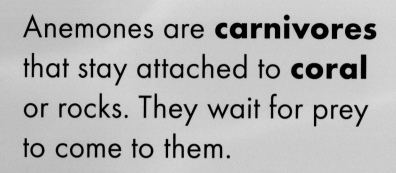

Anemones are **carnivores** that stay attached to **coral** or rocks. They wait for prey to come to them.

Then, they shoot their venom.
It stings and **paralyzes** prey!

Helping Each Other

Mucus protects clownfish from sea anemone venom. This helps clownfish find shelter in sea anemone tentacles.

In return, the fish scare away
unwelcome guests. Predators
learn to keep their distance!

Clownfish also attract prey for anemones to eat. The clownfish are rewarded with leftover scraps!

Tag Team Trades

clownfish

clean up

give protection

provide meals

sea anemones

provide shelter

give protection

provide meals

With every bite, the clownfish remove **parasites** from anemones. They also stir up water to bring more **oxygen** to anemones!

As roommates, clownfish and sea anemones are a good team. They protect each other from danger. They also provide meals for one another.

Their close friendships
last a lifetime!

Glossary

carnivores—animals that only eat meat

coral—a hard material formed from the skeletons of small animals

coral reefs—coral formations in the ocean, often in warm and shallow waters

invertebrates—animals that do not have a backbone

mucus—a slimy substance

omnivores—animals that eat both meat and plants

oxygen—a breathable gas that supports life

paralyzes—makes motionless

parasites—living things that use other living things to survive; parasites harm their hosts.

predators—animals that hunt other animals for food

prey—animals that are hunted by other animals for food

symbiosis—a close relationship between very different living things

tentacles—long, bendable parts of a sea anemone that are attached to the body

venom—a poison a sea anemone makes

To Learn More

AT THE LIBRARY

Cunningham, Kevin. *Clownfish and Sea Anemones*. Ann Arbor, Mich.: Cherry Lake Publishing, 2017.

Hanáčkova, Pavla. *Amazing Animal Friendships: Odd Couples in Nature*. Brighton, England: Salariya, 2017.

Rustad, Martha E. H. *Clown Fish and Sea Anemones Work Together*. Mankato, Minn.: Capstone Press, 2011.

ON THE WEB

FACTSURFER

Factsurfer.com gives you a safe, fun way to find more information.

1. Go to www.factsurfer.com.

2. Enter "clownfish and sea anemones" into the search box.

3. Click the "Surf" button and select your book cover to see a list of related web sites.

Index

The images in this book are reproduced through the courtesy of: Rich Carey, front cover, pp. 4, 5; magnusdeepbelow, front cover (clownfish left), p. 20; sergemi, pp. 6-7; CK Ma, p. 8; Johannes Kornelius, p. 9; Design Pics Inc/ Alamy, p. 10; Global_Pics, p. 11; Offscreen, p. 12; JaysonPhotography, p. 13; Wet Lizard Photography, p. 14; Avalon/ Bruce Coleman Inc/ Alamy, p. 15; HelloRF Zcool, p. 16; Jake Timms/ Alamy, p. 17; Kletr, p. 18 (left); Dan Exton, p. 18 (right); Colin Marshall/ Alamy, p. 19; Aleksey Stemmer, p. 21.